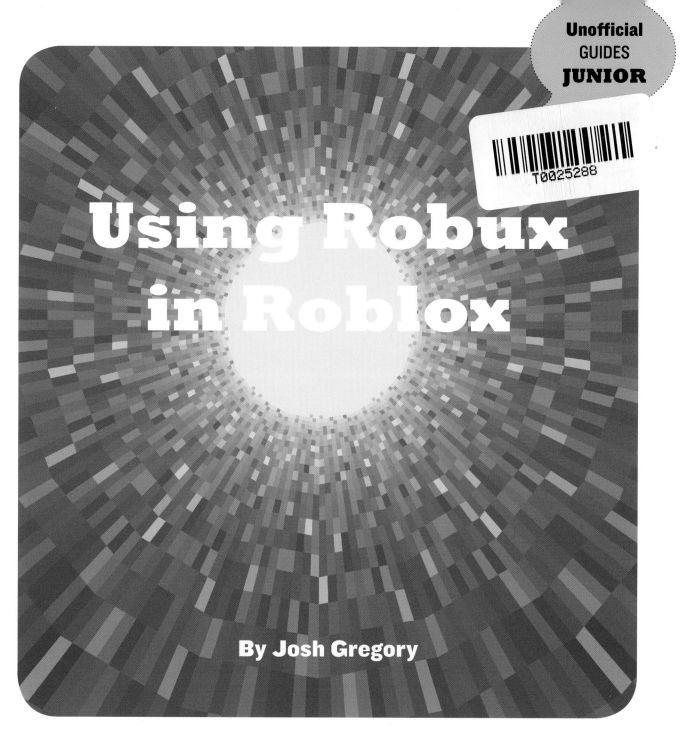

T0025288

Using Robux in Roblox

By Josh Gregory

CHERRY LAKE PRESS

Published in the United States of America by
Cherry Lake Publishing
Ann Arbor, Michigan
www.cherrylakepublishing.com

Reading Adviser: Marla Conn MS, Ed., Literacy specialist, Read-Ability, Inc.

Library of Congress Cataloging-in-Publication Data

Names: Gregory, Josh, author.
Title: Using robux in Roblox / by Josh Gregory.
Description: Ann Arbor, Michigan : Cherry Lake Publishing, 2020. | Series:
   21st century skills innovation library | Includes bibliographical
   references and index. | Audience: Grades 2-3 | Summary: "Roblox is more
   than just a video game. It is a platform where millions of players
   create and share games with each other. With more than 40 million games
   available now and thousands more being added every day, it offers
   players a never ending source of fun and adventure. In this book,
   readers will learn about Robux, the system of in-game currency that
   drives Roblox creations. Includes table of contents, author biography,
   sidebars, glossary, index, and informative backmatter"— Provided by
   publisher.
Identifiers: LCCN 2020010190 | ISBN 9781534169715 (library binding) | ISBN
   9781534171398 (paperback) | ISBN 9781534173231 (pdf) | ISBN
   9781534175075 (ebook)
Subjects: LCSH: Roblox (Computing platform)—Juvenile literature. | Video
   games—Juvenile literature.
Classification: LCC GV1469.35.R594 G746 2020 | DDC 794.8—dc23
LC record available at https://lccn.loc.gov/2020010190

Cherry Lake Publishing would like to acknowledge the work of the Partnership for 21st Century Learning,
a Network of Battelle for Kids. Please visit *http://www.battelleforkids.org/networks/p21* for more information.

Printed in the United States of America
Corporate Graphics

Table of Contents

Some players have created truly amazing things using *Roblox* building tools.

All Kinds of Options

Roblox offers players more options than just about any other video game. Players can choose from millions of different *Roblox* games to play. They can also adjust every detail of their characters' looks. Making these decisions is a big part of the fun. Players express themselves with fun fashions. You can even design your own games and clothing if you get an idea.

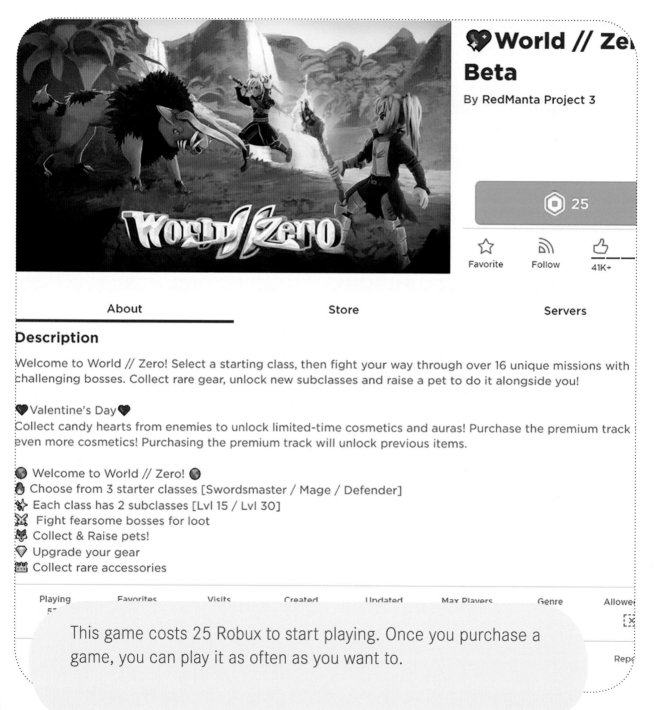

World // Zero Beta

By RedManta Project 3

◉ 25

☆ Favorite   ⋙ Follow   👍 41K+

About   Store   Servers

Description

Welcome to World // Zero! Select a starting class, then fight your way through over 16 unique missions with challenging bosses. Collect rare gear, unlock new subclasses and raise a pet to do it alongside you!

💖Valentine's Day💖
Collect candy hearts from enemies to unlock limited-time cosmetics and auras! Purchase the premium track even more cosmetics! Purchasing the premium track will unlock previous items.

🌐 Welcome to World // Zero! 🌐
🔥 Choose from 3 starter classes [Swordsmaster / Mage / Defender]
🐾 Each class has 2 subclasses [Lvl 15 / Lvl 30]
⚔️ Fight fearsome bosses for loot
🦊 Collect & Raise pets!
🛡️ Upgrade your gear
👑 Collect rare accessories

Playing	Favorites	Visits	Created	Updated	Max Players	Genre	Allowe

This game costs 25 Robux to start playing. Once you purchase a game, you can play it as often as you want to.

What Are Robux?

When you start playing *Roblox*, you only have a few choices for designing your **avatar**. And you might find that you can't play certain games. You'll need some Robux if you want to explore everything *Roblox* has to offer. Robux are *Roblox*'s in-game money. You can use them in all kinds of ways.

Catalog

| | Search | Featured |

Category

Featured › Featured Accessories

Relevance

View All Items

Featured

   All Featured Items

   Featured Accessories

   Featured Animations

   Featured Faces

   Featured Gear

   Featured Bundles

   Featured Emotes

Community
Creations

Collectibles   +

Clothing   —

   All Clothing

   Shirts

   T-Shirts

   Pants

   Bundles

Body Parts   +

Gear   +

Accessories   +

Avatar Animations   +

Filters

Genre

All Genres

☐ Building

☐ Horror

☐ To

☐

☐

Flamingo
By DieSoft
◎ 50

TONK
By TheShipArchit...
◎ 200

Bear Face Mask
◎ 100

Beautiful Hair for Beautiful
◎ 95

Mermaid Princess
By Sukimeki
◎ 130

**Bra...
Pon...**
By B...
◎ 1...

Platinum Space Bun
By Erythia
◎ 130

Evil Red Wings
By TheShipArchit...
◎ 100

Classic Swordpack
◎ 150

Fuzzy Polar Bear Hood
By Beeism
◎ 150

Shimmering Brown French
By Beeism
◎ 150

Holi...
◎ 5...

Midnight Motor

Vintage Glasses

White Luxury Backpack

Sparkling Angel Wings

Black Eagle Wings
By TheShipArchit...
◎ 3...

**Bla...
Bra...**

Items in the catalog have a wide range of prices.

8

Online Shopping

Choose "Catalog" from the main *Roblox* page. Here, you'll see all kinds of clothes, body parts, and other objects. You can spend *Robux* to purchase these items. Then you can use the items to **customize** your avatar. Some things in the catalog are made by the official *Roblox* team. Others are made by players like you!

Tiny Transactions

Most things in the catalog cost just a few Robux each. These are examples of **microtransactions**. Microtransactions are often very cheap. But remember that the costs can add up over time.

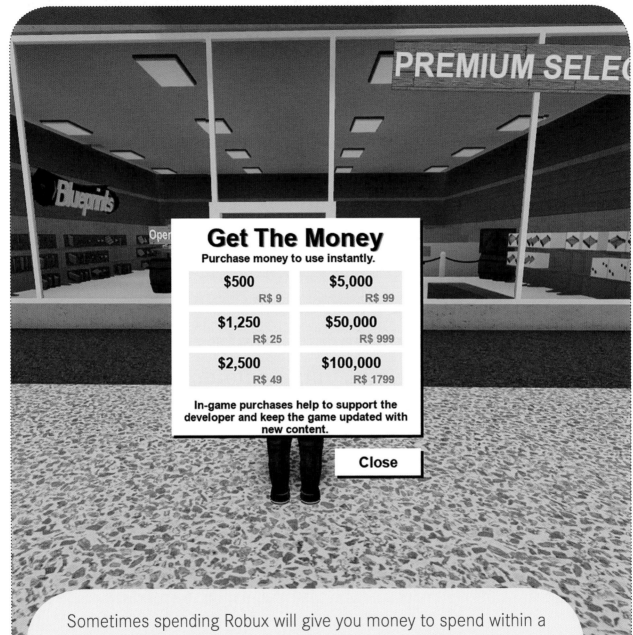

Get The Money

Purchase money to use instantly.

$500 R$ 9	**$5,000** R$ 99
$1,250 R$ 25	**$50,000** R$ 999
$2,500 R$ 49	**$100,000** R$ 1799

In-game purchases help to support the developer and keep the game updated with new content.

Close

Sometimes spending Robux will give you money to spend within a specific *Roblox* game. Here, the Robux cost is listed in green.

In-Game Purchases

You can also spend Robux in most of the millions of games on *Roblox*. Some games require you to pay Robux before you can start playing. Others let you spend Robux to unlock new options during a game. For example, you might buy new cars in a racing game. Or you might buy pets that follow your character around in an adventure game.

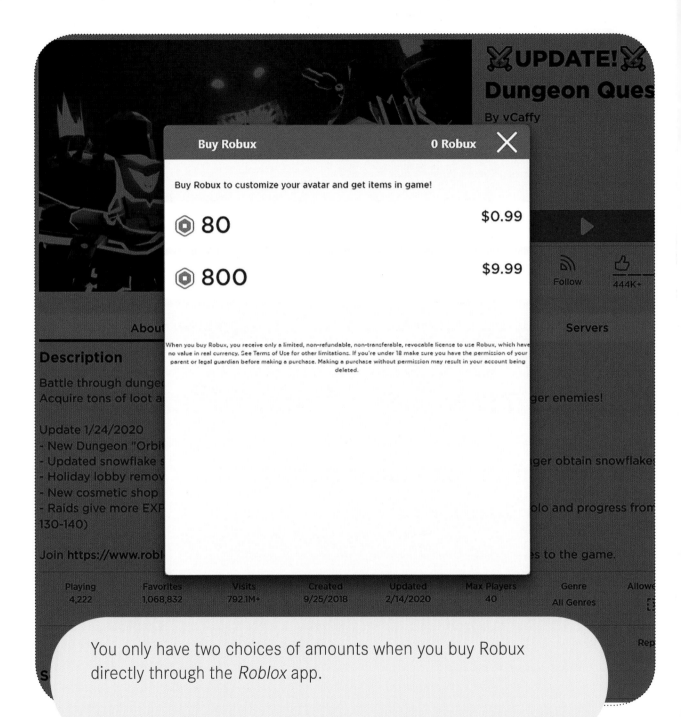

Buy Robux

0 Robux

Buy Robux to customize your avatar and get items in game!

⬢ **80** $0.99

⬢ **800** $9.99

When you buy Robux, you receive only a limited, non-refundable, non-transferable, revocable license to use Robux, which have no value in real currency. See Terms of Use for other limitations. If you're under 18 make sure you have the permission of your parent or legal guardian before making a purchase. Making a purchase without permission may result in your account being deleted.

You only have two choices of amounts when you buy Robux directly through the *Roblox* app.

Buying Robux

You can download *Roblox* and start playing for free. But you'll need to spend real money if you want to use Robux. For $0.99, you can buy 80 Robux directly from the *Roblox* app. Spending $9.99 gets you 800 Robux. You can also buy Robux gift cards from stores or order them online. These come in all kinds of amounts.

Always Ask Permission

Never buy Robux without asking your parents first. You could get in big trouble with your parents for spending too much money. It is also against the official *Roblox* rules.

🅿 Roblox Premium

Joining Roblox Premium gets you a monthly Robux allowance and a 10% bonus when buying Robux. You will also get access to Roblox's economy features including buying, selling, and trading items, as well as increased revenue share on all sales in your games.

$4.99	$9.99	$19.99
◉ **450**	◉ **1000**	◉ **2200**
Buy Now!	Buy Now!	Buy Now!

Even more Features

Get More Robux	Get 10% more when purchasing Robux
Sell More	Resell items and get more Robux selling your creations
Trade	Trade items with other Premium members

Roblox Premium also gives you bonuses if you sell your own creations in the catalog.

A Monthly Allowance

Another way to get Robux is to sign up for a *Roblox* Premium account. This costs $4.99, $9.99, or $19.99 per month. In return, you will get a fresh supply of Robux every month. You will also get a 10 percent discount anytime you decide to buy additional Robux. This can be a good value if you already spend a lot of time and money on *Roblox*.

Anytime you spend Robux in a specific game, you are giving money to that game's creators.

Making Money

Want to earn Robux without spending any real money? Try creating something in *Roblox*. Make a new game. Other players might spend Robux to play it. Or make some clothes for the catalog. Other players might buy them. When other players spend Robux on your creations, you get to keep some of it!

Turning Robux into Cash

Roblox players who are 13 or older can turn their Robux into real money. Some people have even built careers as professional *Roblox* creators.

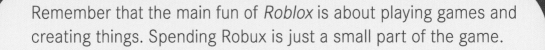

Remember that the main fun of *Roblox* is about playing games and creating things. Spending Robux is just a small part of the game.

Spend Carefully

You should set a **budget** before you start spending Robux. You can't simply buy everything that looks cool. This would cost a lot of money. It would be hard to figure out how much you spent overall. Instead, decide how much you want to spend each week or each month. Then stick to your budget. Don't spend more than your limit, no matter what happens!

You might see other players wearing all kinds of cool gear. But don't spend past your budget just because you want to look like them.

Avoid the Hype

Think hard before you spend your Robux. Are you buying something because you really want it? Or are you buying something because everyone else is doing it? It's easy to get caught up in the excitement of a popular item or game. But it is better to follow your own tastes. There is something for everyone in *Roblox*. Seek out your own style!

Glossary

avatar (AV-uh-tar) a character that represents you in a video game

budget (BUH-jit) a plan for spending a certain amount of money within a period of time

customize (KUS-tuh-myze) change to meet someone's tastes or needs

microtransactions (MYE-kroh-trans-ak-shuhns) things that can be purchased for a small amount of money within a video game or other computer program

Find Out More

Books

Cunningham, Kevin. *Video Game Designer*. Ann Arbor, MI: Cherry Lake Publishing, 2016.

Powell, Marie. *Asking Questions About Video Games*. Ann Arbor, MI: Cherry Lake Publishing, 2016.

Web Sites

Roblox

www.roblox.com

Sign up for a *Roblox* account, download the game, and start playing.

Roblox Support

https://en.help.roblox.com/hc/en-us

Find answers to common questions about *Roblox* and check out some guides to getting started.

Index

About the Author

Josh Gregory is the author of more than 150 books for kids. He has written about everything from animals to technology to history. A graduate of the University of Missouri–Columbia, he currently lives in Chicago, Illinois.